200 Thoughts

Thoughts to awaken your consciousness, stimulate your brain and shake up your paradigm

JENNIFER TOMLIN, B.SC.

BALBOA.PRESS
A DIVISION OF HAY HOUSE

Balboa Press books may be ordered through booksellers or by contacting:

Balboa Press
A Division of Hay House
1663 Liberty Drive
Bloomington, IN 47403
www.balboapress.com
1 (877) 407-4847

Because of the dynamic nature of the Internet, any web addresses or links contained in this book may have changed since publication and may no longer be valid. The views expressed in this work are solely those of the author and do not necessarily reflect the views of the publisher, and the publisher hereby disclaims any responsibility for them.

The author of this book does not dispense medical advice or prescribe the use of any technique as a form of treatment for physical, emotional, or medical problems without the advice of a physician, either directly or indirectly. The intent of the author is only to offer information of a general nature to help you in your quest for emotional and spiritual well-being. In the event you use any of the information in this book for yourself, which is your constitutional right, the author and the publisher assume no responsibility for your actions.

Any people depicted in stock imagery provided by Getty Images are models, and such images are being used for illustrative purposes only. Certain stock imagery © Getty Images.

Print information available on the last page.

ISBN: 978-1-9822-5139-0 (sc)
ISBN: 978-1-9822-5140-6 (e)

Balboa Press rev. date: 07/29/2020

This book is dedicated to Steve,
who has had my back this whole time.

Remember:

There are more things in heaven
and earth, Horatio,
Than are dreamt of in your philosophy.

- Hamlet (1.5.167-8), Hamlet to Horatio

You're in the unknown. And from the unknown, all things are created. You are in the quantum field.

–Joe Dispenza, DC

Peace of mind and a healthy body are inevitable
when you begin to think and feel in the right
way. Whatever you claim mentally and feel
as true, your subconscious mind will accept
and bring forth into your experience.

– C. James Jensen, Author

200 Thoughts

As a person thinks, feels, and believes, so is the
condition of [their] mind, body, and circumstances.

– Joseph Murphy PhD, Psychologist

You are not a drop in the ocean. You
are the entire ocean in a drop.

— Rumi, Poet, Scholar, Theologian

200 Thoughts

If we could change ourselves, the tendencies
in the world would also change. As a man
changes his own nature, so does the attitude
of the world change towards him.

– Mahatma Ghandi

200 Thoughts

...when feelings become the means of thinking,
or if we cannot think greater than how we feel, we
can never change. To change is to think greater
than how we feel. To change is to act greater than
the familiar feelings of the memorized self.

–Joe Dispenza, DC

200 Thoughts

To remove discord, confusion, lack, and
limitation from your life, you must remove
the cause. That cause is the way you use your
conscious mind, the thoughts and images
you encourage in it. Change the cause, and
you change the effect. It's just that simple.

–Joseph Murphy PhD, Psychologist

"As above, so below, as within, so without,
as the universe, so the soul…

- Hermes Trismegistus

The truth is that happiness is a mental and spiritual state. A promotion of external honor will not yield happiness. Your strength, joy, and happiness consist in finding out the law of divine order and right action lodged in your subconscious mind and applying these principles in all phases of your life.

– Joseph Murphy PhD, Psychologist.

Quantum physics thus reveals a
basic Oneness of the Universe

- Erwin Schrodinger

Whatsoever things are true, whatsoever things are honest, whatsoever things are just, whatsoever things are pure, whatsoever things are lovely, whatsoever things are of good report; if there be any virtue, if there be any praise, think on these things.

– PHIL 4:8

The subconscious mind controls 95 percent of our behaviour and gene-regulating cognitive activity through programs obtained primarily from the field of beliefs. When we take command of our own subconscious beliefs and emotions, individually and collectively, we take back creative control over our lives.

– Bruce H. Lipton, PhD

200 Thoughts

The anticipation of consciousness expecting
to see something – the *feeling* that something
is there to see – is the act that creates.

– Gregg Braden, Author

200 Thoughts

If you do not like your experience, then you must change the nature of your conscious thought and expectations. You must alter the kind of messages that you are sending through your thoughts to your own body, to friends and associates.

– Jane Roberts

200 Thoughts

Write it on your heart that every day
is the best day in the year.

– Ralph Waldo Emerson

Our thoughts are mainly controlled by our subconscious, which is largely formed before the age of 6, and you cannot change the subconscious mind by just thinking about it.

– Bruce H. Lipton, PhD

200 Thoughts

A map is not the road.

– Arnold Mindell, PhD, Psychologist

Useful as it is under everyday circumstances
to say that the world exists 'out there'
independent of us, that view can no longer
be upheld. There is a strange sense in
which this is a 'participatory' universe.

— John Wheeler, PhD, Physicist

We are part of this universe; we are in this universe, but perhaps more important than both of those facts, is that the universe is in us.

– Neil dGrasse Tyson, PhD, Astrophysicist

We are stardust, we are golden, and we've
got to get ourselves back to the garden.

– Joni Mitchell, Singer Songwriter

One way or another, a root essence is unfolding you into being who you are and doing what you are doing. Knowing yourself means knowing this root.

– Arnold Mindell, PhD, Psychologist

To the mind that is still, the whole
universe surrenders.

– Lao Tzu

Man's mind, stretched to a new idea, never goes back to its original dimension.

– Oliver Wendell Holmes

The psyche at times functions outside of the spatio-temporal law of causality.

– C. G. Jung, PhD, Psychology, Psychiatry

A human being is part of the whole, called
by us "Universe" – a part limited in time and
space. He experiences himself, his thoughts and
feelings as something separated from the rest –
a kind of optical delusion of consciousness."

Albert Einstein to N. Salit, March 4, 1950. AEA 61-228

We are exquisitely social creatures. Our survival depends on understanding the actions, intentions and emotions of others. Mirror neurons allow us to grasp the minds of other not through conceptual reasoning but through direct stimulation. By feeling – not by thinking.

– Giacomo Rizzolatti, PhD, Neuropsychology

Rather than a universe of static certainty, at the
most fundamental level of matter, the world and
its relationships are uncertain and unpredictable,
a state of pure potential of infinite possibility.

– Lynne McTaggart, Author

My belief is in the blood and flesh as being wiser than the intellect. The body-unconscious is where life bubbles up in us. It is how we know that we are alive, alive to the depths of our souls and in touch somewhere with the vivid reaches of the cosmos.

– D.H. Lawrence

200 Thoughts

What lies behind us and what lies before us are tiny matters compared to what lied *within* us.

– Ralph Waldo Emerson

200 Thoughts

Imagination is more important than
knowledge. Knowledge is limited.
Imagination encircles the world.

Quoted in interview by G.S. Viereck, *The
Saturday Evening Post,*, October 26,1929.

He who conforms to the course of the Tao, following the natural processes of Heaven and Earth, finds it easy to manage the whole world.

– Huai Nan Tzu

What you think, you become. What you feel, you attract. What you imagine, you create.

– The Buddha

200 Thoughts

Words are, in my not so humble opinion, our
most inexhaustible source of magic. Capable
of both inflicting injury, and remedying it.

– Albus Dumbledore

One is led to a new notion of unbroken wholeness which denies the classical idea of analyzability of the world into separately and independently existing parts...We have reversed the usual classical notion that the independent 'elementary parts' of the world are the fundamental reality, and that the various systems are merely particular contingent forms and arrangements of these parts. Rather, we say that inseparable quantum interconnectedness of the whole universe is the fundamental reality, and that relatively independently behaving parts are merely particular and contingent forms within this whole.

– David Bohm, PhD, Theoretical Physics

Time is what prevents everything
from happening at once.

– John Wheeler, PhD, Physicist

What we observe is not nature itself, but nature exposed to our method of questioning.

– Werner Heisenberg, Physicist, Nobel Laureate Physics

Happier thoughts lead to essentially a happier
biochemistry. A happier, healthier body.

– John Hagelin, PhD, Physics

It moves. It moves not. It is far, and It is near. It is within all this, And It is outside of all this.

– The Upanishads

The real revolution that came with Einstein's
theory...was the abandonment of the idea that
the space-time coordinate system has objective
significance as a separate physical entity.
Instead of this idea, relativity theory implies
that the space and time coordinates are only
the elements of a language that is used by
an observer to describe his environment.

– Mendel Sachs, PhD, Theoretical Physics

You are an aperture through which the
universe is looking at and exploring itself.

– Alan Watts, MA Theology

200 Thoughts

As long as we live and think, we will hold images in our minds, and these images develop into the things of our lives, and so long as we think a certain way we must live a certain way, and no amount of willing or wishing will change it, only the vision we carry within.

– U.S. Andersen, Author

Mystics understand the roots of the Tao but not its branches; scientists understand its branches but not its roots. Science does not need mysticism and mysticism does not need science; but man need both.

– Fritjof Capra, PhD, Theoretical Physics

Perhaps the most important, and the most insidious, assumption that we absorb in our childhoods is that of the material world of object existing out there – independent of subjects, who are the observers.

– Amit Goswami, PhD, Theoretical Nuclear Physics

Emotions are the glue that holds the
cells of the organism together.

– Candace Pert, PhD, Pharmacology

Rather than being your thoughts and
emotions, be the awareness behind them.

– Eckhart Tolle, Author

Those who are not shocked when they
first come across quantum theory cannot
possibly have understood it.

– Niels Bohr, PhD, Nobel Laureate Physics

Nature at the quantum level is not a machine that goes its inexorable way. Instead, what answer we get depends on the question we put, the experiment we arrange, the registering device we choose. We are inescapably involved in bringing out that which appears to be happening.

– John Wheeler, PhD, Physicist

My brain is only a receiver, in the Universe there is a core from which we obtain knowledge, strength and inspiration. I have not penetrated into the secrets of this core, but I know that it exists.

– Nikola Tesla, Engineer

Observations are to be regarded as
discrete, discontinuous events. Between
there are gaps which we cannot fill in.

– Erwin Schrodinger, PhD, Nobel Laureate Physics

200 Thoughts

It is within all this. It is outside all this.

– the Upanishads

You and I are all as much continuous
with the physical universe as a wave
is continuous with the ocean.

– Alan Watts, MA Theology

To the liberated, the whole world is family.

– Sanskrit proverb

Make no mistake about it; there is no scientific evidence to support the claim that everything is matter. In fact, there is much evidence to the contrary.

– Amit Goswami, PhD, Theoretical Nuclear Physics

Watch your thoughts; they become words. Watch your words; they become actions. Watch your actions; they become habit. Watch your habits; they become character. Watch your character; it becomes your destiny.

– Lao Tzu

200 Thoughts

I suggest that the body and soul react to each other in sympathy. A change in the state of the soul would necessarily have an effect on the body and vice versa.

– Aristotle

The happiest person is the one who constantly bring forth and practices what is best in himself or herself. Happiness and virtue complement each other. Not only are the best the happiest, but the happiest are usually the best in the art of living life successfully.

– Dr. Joseph Murphy PhD, Psychologist

Do not believe anything simply because you have heart it. Do not believe anything simply because it is spoken and rumoured by many, or merely on the authority of your teachers and elders. But after observation and analysis, when you find anything that agrees with reason, then accept it and live up to it.

– The Buddha

Science cannot solve the ultimate mystery of nature. And that is because, in the last analysis, we ourselves are...part of the mystery that we are trying to solve.

– Max Planck, PhD, Nobel Laureate Physics

200 Thoughts

The law of life is this: all things both good and evil are constructed from an image held in mind.

– U.S. Andersen, Author

Regardless of what we choose to call it or
which laws of physics it may or not conform
to, the field that connects everything
in creation is real. It's here in this very
instant – it exists as you and as me.

– Gregg Braden, Author

Imagination creates reality...
Man is all imagination.

– Neville

As far as the laws of mathematics refer to reality, they are not certain; and as far as they are certain, they do not refer to reality." From "Geometry and Experience," an address to the Prussian Academy of Sciences, Berlin, January 27, 1921

200 Thoughts

We are the mirror as well as the face in it.

– Rumi, Poet, Scholar, Theologian

The kingdom of god is within you.

– Luke 17:21

200 Thoughts

Life is a mirror and will reflect back to
the thinker what he thinks into it.

– Ernest Holmes, PhD, Philosophy

…whether you've been trying to effect positive change to create a new state of being or you've been running on autopilot and staying stuck in the same old state of being, the truth is that you've always been your own placebo.

– Dr. Joe Dispenza, DC

200 Thoughts

It's not the strongest of the species that survives,
nor the most intelligent that survives. It is
the one that is most adaptable to change.

– Charles Darwin

Facts which at first seem improbably will, even on scant explanation, drop the cloak which has hidden them and stand forth in naked and simple beauty.

– Galileo

200 Thoughts

Until we attach a significance of our own
making to the outcome, each experience is
simply an opportunity to express ourselves…
nothing more and nothing less.

– Gregg Braden, Author

To study the Way is to study the self. To study the self is to forget the self. To forget the self is to be enlightened by all things.

– Dogen

200 Thoughts

The atoms or elementary particles themselves...
form a world of potentialities or possibilities
rather than one of things or facts.

– Werner Heisenberg, Physicist, Nobel Laureate Physics

Human beings can alter their lives by
altering their attitudes of mind.

– William James, PhD, Psychology, Philosophy

We're creators – and even more than that, we're connected creators. Through the Divine Matrix, we participate in the constant change that gives meaning to life. The question now is less about whether or not we're passive observers and more about how we can intentionally create.

– Gregg Braden, Author

When you live your life with an appreciation of coincidences and their meanings, you connect with the underlying field of infinite possibilities.

– William James, PhD, Psychology, Philosophy

Men often become what they believe themselves to be. If I believe I cannot do something, it makes me incapable of doing it. But when I believe I can, then I acquire the ability to do it even if I didn't have it in the beginning.

– Mahatma Ghandi

Everything emerges and returns to a fundamental
field of information that connects us all

- Nassim Haramein

Everything can be taken from a man
but the last of human freedoms – to
choose one's attitude in any given set of
circumstances, to choose one's own way.

– Viktor Frankl, PhD, Neurology, Psychiatry

When you reach the end of what
you should know, you will be at the
beginning of what you should sense.

– Kahlil Gibran, Poet, Artist

200 Thoughts

What we think determines what happens
to us, so if we want to change our lives,
we need to stretch our minds.

– Wayne Dyer, Author

You can never teach a man anything. You can only help him to discover it within himself.

– Galileo

Act as if what you do makes a difference. It does.

– William James, PhD, Psychology, Philosophy

Things are as they are. Looking out into the universe at night, we make no comparisons between right and wrong stars, nor between well and badly arranged constellations.

– Alan Watts, MA Theology

200 Thoughts

They must often change, who would be
constant in happiness or wisdom.

– Confucius

We are shaped by our thoughts; we become
what we think. When the mind is pure, joy
follows like a shadow that never leaves.

– The Buddha

But when you finally discover me, the one
naked Truth arisen from within, Absolute
Awareness permeates the Universe.

– Yeshe Tsogyel

The fundamental process of Nature lies
outside space-time but generates events
that can be located in space-time.

– Henry Stapp, PhD, Mathematical Physics

Consciousness is a singular for
which there is no plural.

– Erwin Schrodinger, PhD, Nobel Laureate Physics

The most fundamental element of reality is the quantum vacuum, the energy- and in-formation-filled plenum that underlies, generates, and interacts with our universe, and with whatever universes may exist in the Metaverse.

– Ervin Laszlo, Author

This universe is not outside of you. Look inside yourself; everything that you want, you already are.

– Rumi, Poet, Scholar, Theologian

200 Thoughts

All that we are is a result of what we have thought, it is founded on our thoughts and made up of our thoughts.

– The Buddha

200 Thoughts

In the history of the collective as in the
history of the individual, everything depends
on the development of consciousness.

– C. G. Jung, PhD, Psychology, Psychiatry

I have...no hesitation in declaring quite bluntly
that the acceptance of a really existing material
world, as the explanation of the fact that we all
find in the end that we are empirically in the
same environment, is mystical and metaphysical.

– Erwin Schrodinger, PhD, Nobel Laureate Physics

Behind every atom of this world
hides an infinite universe.

– Rumi, Poet, Scholar, Theologian

Everyday reality is just one provincial way of perceiving the world. There are others that are equally valid, and it's in some of those worlds where the supernormal resides.

– Dean Radin, PhD, Educational Psychology

A miracle does not happen in contradiction
to nature, but in contradiction to that
which is known to us of nature.

– Saint Augustine

We must bear in mind that what was mystical a thousand years ago is no longer so, and what is mysterious now may become lawfully intelligible a hundred years hence. It is the Infinite, the Ocean of Power, that is at the back of all manifestations.

– Swami Yogananda

There are beautiful and wild forces within us.

– St. Francis of Assisi

The infinite intelligence within your subconscious
mind can reveal to you everything you need to
know at every moment of time and point of space
provided you are open minded and receptive.

– C. James Jensen, Author

The mind is the matrix of all matter.

– Max Planck, PhD, Nobel Laureate Physics

In the last count matter is but a waveform disturbance in the quasi-infinite energy- and in-formation sea that is the connecting field, and the enduring memory, of the universe.

– Ervin Laszlo, Author

We are part of a universe that is a work in progress. We are tiny patches of the universe looking at itself, and building itself.

– John Wheeler, PhD, Physicist

200 Thoughts

When we peer into the void of the universe in search of its limits, or into the quantum world of the atom, the very act of us looking puts something there for us to see.

– Gregg Braden, Author

Beauty is eternity gazing at itself in a mirror.
But you are eternity and you are the mirror.

– Kahlil Gibran, Poet, Artist

Science is the contemporary language of mysticism.

– Dr. Joe Dispenza, DC

You are the universe in ecstatic motion.

– Rumi, Poet, Scholar, Theologian

Our normal waking consciousness, rational consciousness as we call it, is but one special type of consciousness, whilst all about it, parted from it by the flimsiest of screens, there lie potential forms of consciousness entirely different.

– William James, PhD, Psychology, Philosophy

200 Thoughts

Perhaps the only limits to the human
mind are those we believe in.

– Willis Harman, PhD

Under the influence of love, the membrane
of individuality becomes porous.

– Susanne Langer

200 Thoughts

Creativity comes from the spiritual realm, the collective consciousness. And the mind is in a different realm that the molecules of the brain. The brain is a receiver, not a source.

– Candace Pert, PhD, Pharmacology

We must become in our lives the very things
that we choose to experience in the world.

— Gregg Braden, Author

200 Thoughts

When you lose touch with inner stillness, you lose touch with yourself. When you lose touch with yourself, you lose yourself in the world. Your innermost sense of self, of who you are, is inseparable from stillness.

– Eckhart Tolle, Author

Everything in the universe is within
you. Ask all from yourself.

– Rumi, Poet, Scholar, Theologian

Space and time are two of the most fundamental classical concepts, but according to quantum mechanics they are secondary. The entanglements are primary. They interconnect quantum systems without reference to space and time.

– Vladko Vedral, PhD, Physics

You are that vast thing that you see
far, far off with great telescopes.

– Alan Watts, MA Theology

In addition to our immediate consciousness,
which is of a thoroughly personal nature...
there exists a second psychic system of a
collective, universal, and impersonal nature
which is identical in all individuals.

– C. G. Jung, PhD, Psychology, Psychiatry

Everything in the universe is within you. Ask all from yourself.

— Rumi, Poet, Scholar, Theologian

Happiness does not depend on what you have or who you are. It solely relies on what you think.

– The Buddha

200 Thoughts

If you correct your mind, the rest of
your life will fall into place.

– Lao Tzu

The quantum field responds not to what we want; it responds to who we are being.

— Dr. Joe Dispenza, DC

Nothing ever exists entirely alone; everything
is in relation to everything else.

– The Buddha

Can you accept the notion that once you change your internal state, you don't need the external world to provide you with a reason to feel joy, gratitude, appreciation, or any other elevated emotion?

– Dr. Joe Dispenza, DC

Shine like the whole universe is yours.

– Rumi, Poet, Scholar, Theologian

So if we want to change some aspect of our reality, we have to think, feel and act in new ways; we have to "be" different in terms of our responses to experiences. We have to "become" someone else. We have to create a new state of mind...we need to observe a new outcome with that new mind.

– Dr. Joe Dispenza, DC

You are here to enable the divine purpose of the Universe to unfold. That is how important you are!

– Eckhart Tolle, Author

I regard consciousness as fundamental. I regard matter as derivative from consciousness. We cannot get behind consciousness. Everything that we talk about, everything that we regard as existing, postulates consciousness.

– Max Planck, PhD, Nobel Laureate Physics

200 Thoughts

It is my personal opinion that in the science of the future reality with neither be 'psychic' nor 'physical' but somehow both and somehow neither.

– Wolfgang Pauli, PhD, Nobel Laureate Physics

Awake. Be the witness of your thoughts. You are what observes, not what you observe.

– The Buddha

Is it possible that consciousness, like space-time, has its own intrinsic degrees of freedom, and that neglecting these will lead to a description of the universe that is fundamentally incomplete? What if our perceptions are as real, or maybe in a certain sense, are even more real, than material objects?

– Andrei Linde, PhD, Theoretical Physics

200 *Thoughts*

Perhaps consciousness plays an equally important role in nature, despite the fact that it has been ignored until now in understanding well-studied physical processes in the brain and elsewhere.

– Alan Wallace, Author

Like gravity, in the small scale it's too weak to be noticed...it's too alien to our ordinary way of viewing the objective world to detect. But it might be the glue that holds everything together and creates something rather than nothing.

– Dean Radin, PhD, Educational Psychology

What you seek is seeking you.

– Rumi, Poet, Scholar, Theologian

What you think, you become. What you feel,
you attract. What you imagine, you create.

– The Buddha

You are powerful enough to influence
matter because at the most elementary
level, you are energy with a consciousness.
You are mindful matter.

– Dr. Joe Dispenza, DC

Thou art that.

– The Upanishads

If the mind is intensely eager, everything
can be accomplished. Mountains
can be crumbled into atoms.

– Vivekananda

The soul can never be cut into pieces by any weapon, nor can it be burned by fire, nor moistened by water, nor withered by the wind.

– Bhagavad Gita 2.23

Develop the inner vision and the habit of
listening to the inner Voice; and you are
assured of unshakable Peace and infinite Joy.

– Atharva Veda

Luminous beings are we...Not this crude matter.

– Master Yoda

200 Thoughts

The cosmos is all that is or ever was or ever will be. Our feeblest contemplations of the cosmos stir us – there is a tingling in the spine, a catch in the voice, a faint sensation, as if I distant memory, or falling from a height. We know we are approaching the greatest of mysteries.

– Carl Sagan, PhD, Astrophysics

Look up at the stars and not down at your feet.
Try to make sense of what you see, and wonder
about what makes the universe exist. Be curious.

– Stephen Hawking, PhD, Theoretical Physics

If the evolution of knowledge in this century exceeds that of the last, which seems likely, then we can look forward to a future that's likely to redefine our concepts of reality far beyond any of the strangest concepts we've encountered so far.

— Dean Radin, PhD, Educational Psychology

200 Thoughts

With our thoughts, we make the world.

– The Buddha

The untrained mind, the natural state of
human consciousness, has very little free
will. We talk about free will, about freedom
of choice, but without training the mind, we
don't truly have the ability to choose.

– Noah Levine, Author

Everything we call real is made of things
that cannot be regarded as real.

– Niels Bohr, PhD, Nobel Laureate Physics,
PhD, Nobel Laureate Physics

Truly, you're here because a lot of stars blew up.

– Rick Hanson, Author

The Buddhist does not believe in an independent
or separately existing external world, into
whose dynamic forces he could insert himself.
The external world and his inner world are
for him only two sides of the same fabric,
in which the threads of all forces and of all
events, of all forms of consciousness and of
their objects, are woven into an inseparable net
of endless, mutually conditioned relations.

– Lama Anagarika Govinda

I am larger, better than I thought, I did
not know I held so much goodness.

– Walt Whitman

Do all that you can, with all that you have, in the time that you have, in the place where you are.

– Nkosi Johnson

200 Thoughts

We are in the universe and the universe is in us.

– Neil dGrasse Tyson, PhD, Astrophysicist

Quantum physics shows us the universe
as a dynamic web of connection.

– Robert Moss, Author

When we measure something we are forcing
an undetermined, undefined world to
assume an experimental value. We are not
measuring the world, we are creating it.

– Niels Bohr, PhD, Nobel Laureate Physics,
PhD, Nobel Laureate Physics

200 Thoughts

Quantum physics thus reveals a
basic oneness of the universe.

– Erwin Schrodinger, PhD, Nobel Laureate Physics

In a quantum universe, magic is not
the exception but the rule.

— Arjuna Ardagh, Author

Mathematics is the language with which
God has written the universe.

- Galileo Galilei

Spiritual energy flows in and produces
effects in the phenomenal world.

– William James, PhD, Psychology, Philosophy

200 Thoughts

Your mind takes its shape gradually from
what you routinely rest your mind upon.

– Rick Hanson, Author

Constant dripping hollows out a stone.

– Lucretius

If you want to find the secrets of the universe,
think in terms of energy, frequency and vibration.

– Nikola Tesla, Engineer

Consciousness is the agency that collapses
the wave of a quantum object, which
exists in potential, making it an immanent
particle in the world of manifestation.

– Amit Goswami, PhD, Theoretical Nuclear Physics

You must never be fearful about what
you are doing when it is right.

– Rosa Parks

200 Thoughts

I think more like a quantum Buddhist, in that there is a universal proto-conscious mind which we access, and can influence us. But it actually exists at the fundamental level of the universe, at the Planck scale.

– Stuart Hameroff, MD

200 Thoughts

Man becomes what he thinks about.

– Morris Goodman, PhD, Chemistry

200 Thoughts

For us believing physicists, the demarcation between past, present, and future has merely the significance of but a persistent illusion."

Albert Einstein to Vero Besso and Bice Jahn-Rusconi Besso, March 21, 1955. AEA 7-245

What I thought was unreal now, for me, seems in some ways to be more real than what I think to be real, which seems now to be unreal.

— Fred Alan Wolf, PhD, Theoretical Physics

Inner happiness actually is the fuel of success.

– John Hagelin, PhD, Physics

The eternal present is the space within which your whole life unfolds, the one factor that remains constant. Life is now. There was never a time when your life was not now, nor will there ever be.

– Eckhart Tolle, Author

You are the universe, expressing itself
as a human for a little while.

– Eckhart Tolle, Author

No phenomenon is a real phenomenon
until it is an observed phenomenon.

– John Wheeler, PhD, Physicist

[Quantum mechanics] describes nature as absurd from the point of view of common sense. And yet it fully agrees with experiment. So I hope you can accept nature as she is – absurd.

– Richard Feynman, PhD, Nobel Laureate Physics

All experiences are preceded by mind, having mind as their master, created by mind.

– the Buddha

Your brain simulates the world – each of us lives
in a virtual reality that's close enough to the real
thing that we don't bump into the furniture.

– Rick Hanson, Author

A disciplined mind bring happiness.

– the Buddha

200 Thoughts

I, a universe of atoms, an atom in the universe.

– Richard Feynman, PhD, Nobel Laureate Physics

What one man calls God, another
calls the laws of physics.

– Nikola Tesla, Engineer

Quantum physics tells us that nothing that
is observed is unaffected by the observer.
That statement, from science, holds an
enormous and powerful insight. It means
that everyone sees a different truth, because
everyone is creating what they see.

– Neale Donald Walsch, Author

You are more than your thoughts, your body, or your feelings. You are a swirling vortex of limitless potential who is here to shake things up and create something new that the universe has never seen.

– Richard Bartlett, ND

In order to more fully understand this
reality, we must take into account other
dimensions of a broader reality.

– John Wheeler, PhD, Physicist

Energy, like you, has no beginning
and no end. It can never be destroyed.
It is only ever shifting states.

– Panache Desai

200 Thoughts

Imagination is more important than
knowledge. Knowledge is limited.
Imagination encircles the world.

Quoted in interview by G.S. Viereck,
The Saturday Evening Post,, October 26,1929.

What quantum physics teaches us is that
everything we thought was physical is not physical.

– Bruce H. Lipton, PhD

200 Thoughts

What we know is a drop, what we
don't know is an ocean.

– Isaac Newton

Life is strong and fragile. It's a paradox…It's both things, like quantum physics; It's a particle and a wave at the same time. It all exists all together.

– Joan Jett

And a new philosophy emerged called quantum physics, which suggest that the individual's function is to inform and be informed. You really exist only when you're in a field sharing and exchanging information. You create the realities you inhabit.

– Timothy Leary

As far as the laws of mathematics refer to reality, they are not certain; and as far as they are certain, they do not refer to reality." From "Geometry and Experience," an address to the Prussian Academy of Sciences, Berlin, January 27, 1921.

Even when I was studying mathematics, physics, and computer science, it always seemed that the problem of consciousness was about the most interesting problem out there for science to come to grips with.

— David Chalmers, Author

When our behaviours match our intentions, when our actions are equal to our thoughts, when our minds and our bodies are working together, when our words and our deeds are aligned...there is an immense power behind any individual.

– Dr. Joe Dispenza, DC

Living consciousness somehow is the influence that turns the possibility of something into something real. The most essential ingredient in creating our universe is the consciousness that observes it.

– Lynne McTaggart, Author

200 Thoughts

Awareness of the inner body is consciousness
remembering its origin and returning to the Source.

– Rumi, Poet, Scholar, Theologian

200 Thoughts

The key to growth is the introduction of higher dimensions of consciousness into our awareness.

– Lao Tzu

Consciousness is the process of creating a model of the world using multiple feedback loops in various parameters (e.g. in temperature, space, time, and in relation to others), in order to accomplish a goal (e.g. find mates, food, shelter).

- Michio Kaku

200 Thoughts

We are a way for the cosmos to know itself.

– Carl Sagan, PhD, Astrophysics

What is the Universe? The Universe is a symphony of vibrating strings...We are nothing but Melodies. We are nothing but Cosmic Music played out on vibrating strings and Membranes.

- Michio Kaku

Peace comes from within. Do not seek it without.

– the Buddha

Modern physics has confirmed most dramatically one of the basic ideas of Eastern mysticism; that all the concepts we use to describe nature are limited, that they are not features of reality, as we tend to believe, but creations of the mind; parts of the map, not the territory.

– Fritjof Capra, PhD, Theoretical Physics

200 Thoughts

Wealth is ultimately nothing more than a subconscious conviction on the part of the individual. You will not become a millionaire by saying, *"I am a millionaire, I am a millionaire."* You will grow into a wealth consciousness by building into your mentality the idea of wealth and abundance.

– Dr. Joseph Murphy PhD, Psychologist

The right way to wholeness is made up of fateful detours and wrong turnings.

– C. G. Jung, PhD, Psychology, Psychiatry

200 Thoughts

To be empowered – to be free, to be unlimited,
to be creative, to be genius, to be divine
– that is who you are...Once you feel this
way, memorize this feelings; remember
this feeling. This is who you really are.

– Dr. Joe Dispenza, DC

200 Thoughts

Perhaps the fabric of reality is woven from the woof of matter/energy and the warp of the mind. And when those threads are examined very closely, we find that they don't consist of ordinary stuff. They are made out of pure information.

– Dean Radin, PhD, Educational Psychology

The subconscious mind is the product of universal consciousness, universal knowledge, and universal beauty. It is the reflecting mirror of our conscious mind. The subconscious mind is always eager to manifest through our conscious mind."

- Debasish Mridha

Your vision will become clear only when
you look into your heart. Who looks outside,
dreams. Who looks inside, awakens.

– C. G. Jung, PhD, Psychology, Psychiatry

200 Thoughts

If you are quiet enough, you will hear
the flow of the universe. You will feel
its rhythm. Go with this flow.'

– The Buddha

200 Thoughts

If you get the inside right, the
outside will fall into place.

– Eckhart Tolle, Author

Spacetime tells matter how to move; matter tells spacetime how to curve.

– John Wheeler, PhD, Physicist

Printed in the United States
By Bookmasters